COYOTE HUNTING

The Complete Book: From Head to Tail

Phil Simonski

COYOTE HUNTING
The Complete Book: From Head to Tail

Phil Simonski

Copyright 1994 by Phil Simonski

Sixth Printing, New Revised Edition, November 2005
Fifth Printing, New Revised Edition, May 2003
Fourth Printing, New Revised Edition, June 2000
Third Printing, Revised Edition, February 1998
Second Printing, November 1995
First Printing, December 1994

ISBN 0-912299-59-2

STONEYDALE PRESS PUBLISHING COMPANY
523 Main Street • Box 188
Stevensville, Montana 59870
Phone: 406-777-2729

DEDICATION

To my lovely wife,
Danae,

And children,
Michelle, Yvonne, Suzette and, of course, Rene,
who all suffered hours of cold and wet
to be with Daddy on his expeditions.

ACKNOWLEDGEMENTS

The first printing of *Coyote Hunting: The Complete Book From Head to Tail* was in December 1994. Since that time the art and science of coyote hunting has expanded by leaps and bounds. The book was the first written for the beginner. This updated version was done with much help from publisher Dale Burk and experts in the field such as Gerald Stewart, Bob Blair, Ray Johnson and many others.

My thanks also to Mary Lou Russ, who tackled the task of editing this creation. Her payment was the easiest part — a guided bass fishing trip to Brownlee Reservoir.

Finally and most of all, I want to thank my wife, Danae, for her wholehearted support — again. She answered phone calls, told the fishermen that the crappies were still biting, and shipped caller tapes to eager hunters while I wrote the update on this book.

Phil Simonski

Preface

Man has always been at the top of the food chain. During the Stone Age, developing subspecies learned to survive or became extinct. The species that survived with man during this development learned to adjust. The problem in the last fifty years or so is that technology has increased at such a rapid pace that some critters are having a hard time adjusting. Of course, the other factor, and by far the most important for many, is that their habitat is rapidly disappearing. The hypercritical factor is that urban residents have little knowledge of wildlife management and the dynamics of animal populations. Animal populations that can adjust to new surroundings quickly, like the coyote, just keep growing.

Since the late 1980's fur has become less fashionable and coyotes, being the adaptable animal they are, have expanded their population and ranges. Soon after the first printing of this book began selling back in the eastern United States, I received phone calls from hunters in Maryland, New York and even Florida, states in which I had no idea the coyote even existed.

When I was growing up in Pennsylvania there were no coyotes in that state. I can remember seeing one red fox in upper Bucks County, but that was the wildest canine I ever saw until a trip west in 1958. At that time I was introduced to the western coyote and a forty-plus year love affair started.

The equipment, tactics and other methods in this book are a compilation of those forty years. They reflect practically everything to do with authentic coyote hunting information. One of the most challenging things about hunting coyotes is that the species is very adaptive. No longer are they the symbol of the rural West. Coyotes are found from downtown Los Angeles to the wilds of northern New Jersey, within sight of the Empire State Building. As they change, so must the hunter. The update of this book is information that present technology has to offer to the present day hunter.

This book provides all the pertinent data about the latest techniques for hunting coyotes, be they city dwellers or the old timberline dogs at 8,000 feet. It provides information on how techniques for taking these animals vary depending on their habitat, the time of year and their food source. (You may be surprised to learn they survive very well on house cat and small dogs.)

Yote welcomes you.

Table of Contents

The author with a portion of his 1993 pelts.

Foreword

The late October afternoon is unusually warm and bright on the Oregon high desert as I huddle in a patch of pungent sage and something with a lot of thorns.

Off to the southwest twenty yards, the sounds of a dying rabbit squawk helpless for several moments over a rise in the lava and basalt-studded soil.

Then it is quiet.

"Stand up and shoot, Bill!" shouts Phil Simonski of Baker City, Oregon. He is about equal distance from the speaker, but to the right of my position by forty yards armed with a rifle, but the cagey coyote has sped past him and is now between us, trying to see whether it has any competition for the simulated dying dinner.

With me directly in line behind the coyote, Simonski has no shot, so he stands and yells.

The coyote wheels and runs straight for me.

I get off the first shot at maybe twenty yards, no further, but somehow miss as the coyote accelerates. The second shot is in the dust behind the dog's foot and the third shot is only wishful frustration as the coyote puts distance between us as light speed.

Simonski, who's seen it before, is on his knees laughing.

"You won't get it any closer than that!" he says. "How in the world did you miss a twenty yard shot?"

He will, of course, remind me for years to come that one of Oregon's best wing shots was humiliated before his very eyes.

I think he is just irritated about losing the twenty-five bucks the hide would have brought.

*I read the first printing of Simonski's book, "**Coyote Hunting: The Complete Book From Head To Tail,**" a couple of years ago and was stunned to find detailed in print all of my coyote hunting secrets.*

Plus more than a few new ones I didn't know.

As more and more hunters look elsewhere for places to pursue their passion and prey to stalk, coyotes are getting increased attention. In fact, some guides make seasonal money guiding clients to coyotes out of Bend, Burns, Baker City and other eastern Oregon communities.

A coyote hunt offers all the qualities they are seeking — cunning, excitement, the need to outfox the quarry, easy access on public lands, no limit or tag required beyond a hunting license, and plenty of magnificent scenery.

Simonski is the fox in the coyote's hen house.

He, too, is cunning, exciting and tough to outfox.

And his book is filled with anecdotes (not mine), tips and downright outrageous techniques.

It's a critter you can hunt all year, according to the boss.

But don't ever, ever miss one in front of him.

Bill Monroe
Outdoor Editor, The Oregonian

Introduction

The suggested methods in this book are collected from more than forty years of experience. A true hunter learns by making mistakes; the animal he is hunting never or seldom has a chance to learns from his.

As a young lad living in Philadelphia, I never in my wildest dreams realized I would spend all of my adulthood living in the wide open expanses of eastern Oregon. Since 1958 I have considered myself a resident of this truly remarkable land. Hunting eastern game such as cottontail rabbits, grey squirrels, ruffed grouse, ring-necked pheasants and, of course, whitetail deer are some of my fondest memories. My father was an avid hunter of all kinds of game other than waterfowl. Game and fish were also a part of our diet, even in Philadelphia.

On my eleventh birthday I received a Stevens over and under 22/410. I had long owned a Benjamin air pistol, which the starlings and English sparrows learned to avoid. My first real game, a cottontail, succumbed to the Stevens on opening day of the small game season when I was twelve years old. About that time I also became the proud owner of a converted Japanese 6.5mm. My father, being something of a gunsmith, rechambered and rebored the World War II sniper rifle into a .257 Roberts. That winter of my twelve birthday I saw my first deer hang from the tripod. Those early hunting days are great memories. My dad passed away when I was fourteen. My

The author with a coyote that came to his electronic call.

mother remarried and we moved to the country about twenty-five miles northwest of Philadelphia. I was in heaven. Rabbits and pheasants were abundant in Bucks County at that time. I learned that waterfowl was excellent eating and fairly plentiful. Deer hunting had to be put on hold until I graduated from high school and attended Pennsylvania State University in central Pennsylvania. There, the "oak barrens" were full of deer and even during my freshmen year I managed to hunt. Hunting became an obsession while I was in college and was almost my demise my senior year.

After accepting a permanent position with the U.S. Forest Service, I got married and spent two years in Germany during the building of the Berlin Wall. Germany's approach to wildlife management was very interesting to me. The control of all kinds of critters by "foresters" was the accepted practice. The main purpose was to keep game populations healthy and

Here's some coyote, fox and bobcat pelts taken by the author in a recent season using the techniques outlined in this book. Please see Chapter Nine to learn how to properly care for the pelts.

to provide recreation for the folks who could afford to take part in the sport. The animals, just as here, belong to the state. The difference is that here, once they are taken, they become the hunter's property. In Germany, they still belong to the State with the exception of the trophy head.

During my Forest Service career I continued to hunt, but as my family grew, critters like grouse and trout were a great deal more important to me than that flea bitten critter in the next hay pasture. As my children began to further their education and move away, hunting became less of a necessity. The drive to put food on the table decreased and I turned my attention to competitive bass fishing.

While on a tour of duty as project leader and timber planner on the Fremont National Forest in south central Oregon, I met Ray Johnson. Ray was an avid hunter and fishermen. We had a great deal in common. During that time Ray taught me there are two kinds of coyote pursuers. One is called a coyote shooter; the other, a coyote hunter. There is a world of difference between the two. Up to that point my experience with coyote hunting was mostly that they were shot when hunting other types of game.

Sometimes ranchers contract for the shooting of an individual animal that is killing his livestock. That is done by a coyote hunter. This book is strictly for the coyote hunter, a difference which will become very apparent in the next few chapters.

I had killed my first coyote during the summer of 1959. I was a "JF" (junior forester) on the Paulina Ranger District of the Ochoco National Forest in central Oregon. It seemed that every day going to and from work, marking timber on the Big Happy timber sale, we would see coyotes. My desire to kill one of these critters became overpowering. I carried a .22 pistol, a double action H&R, for about a week until one September afternoon, a young pup of the year decided he wanted to take a close look at the new green Jeep 4x4 that we drove. The shot was less than thirty feet. With the blade of the front sight level with the notch of the rear sight and lined up just behind the front shoulder, I squeezed the first shot. Off went Mr. Coyote without as much as a flinch. The next six rounds were pulled off double action and pointed in the general direction of the rapidly departing coyote. About 100 yards from the jeep the critter all of a sudden turned into a rolling ball of fur; then, it lay still. Retrieving my prize started my education about coyotes.

For a long time I was a coyote shooter. Then, in 1975, Ray took me on my first real coyote hunt. With a great deal of emotion, he tried to impress upon me all the do's and don'ts

Good hunting ethics require respect for landowners' property. One way to form that relationship is by building and using fence stiles. Here is a full equipped coyote hunter using a stile to cross a five-wire fence. Without the stile, this hunter would have a difficult time crossing a tight five-wire fence with shooting sticks, howler, electric caller, rifle, fannypack and, on the way back, hopefully, a coyote. Build a stile or two on a farmer's property and you'll probably have a place to hunt for life.

associated with coyote hunting. At that time coyote pelts were worth upwards to $100 each. Most averaged around $50 to $60. I will never forget our first setup. We were in a small grove of junipers trees, a high spot in a sage brush flat, just east of Hart Mountain Antelope Refuge. The likely direction from which the animals would appear was the east. Ray took a position so he could cover that segment of open sage. My position was facing northwest. About 200 yards away was a juniper covered ridge, and a small draw ran from that ridge angling from Rays' left to my right. About five minutes into the call I had a feeling that something was watching me. I slowly rolled my eyes to my left and looked eyeball to eyeball with a very alive and very nervous coyote. The first thing he did was growl. If I can hear any wild critter growl he is too, too close. I slowly started to lift my gun to the shooting

Deer provide a sizable prey base for the coyote almost anywhere they're found, and while coyotes most often seek out smaller prey, like rabbits and ground squirrels, etc., they can very handily take down a deer like one of these in this herd of mule deer.

position. With the first slight movement this critter was in high gear. All I remember was pointing the K Hornet in the general direction of the fleeing 'yote. When I pulled the trigger, he shifted into the next higher gear. By this time Ray had turned around and was operating without coyote fever. The coyote rolled less than thirty yards from my position. I was hooked. Although I was still trembling, I had caught that terrible disease, called coyote (buck) fever. That day produced four more coyotes.

When I moved from southcentral Lake County to the sprawling metropolis of Baker, Oregon, I became less interested in game hunting and more engrossed with this exceptionally intelligent member of the dog family. From 1985 to the present about the only hunting I have done is for coyotes.

Although I still occasionally roll a mule deer for the freezer when I'm lucky enough to draw a tag, my major effort from early October until the coyote breeding season, which generally starts in mid-February, is calling these critters.

Baker County has proved to be a great place to learn the art of coyote hunting. There are many friendly ranchers who will bend over to help you put some of those dogs in the dirt.

All my experiences related in this book occurred in eastern Oregon. From conversations with other hunters, in other parts of the United States, I believe the principles described here can be made to fit any situation in any location in the North American continent. It won't make any difference if you're hunting those big fifty and sixty pound critters in the central Pennsylvania and New England or the small 'yotes of the desert southwest.

When small mammals become hard to find, full-grown deer and antelope become food for coyotes.

Chapter One

A LITTLE ABOUT THE CRITTER

Before any hunter goes forth and tries to be successful he should learn a little about the animal he is hunting. Its like hunting pheasants in a asphalt parking lot. Do not start looking for many if the habitat is not there. There are darn few pheasants in that parking lot. Coyotes are very adaptable, but they still need water, food and cover.

Coyotes are the most widely distributed member of the genus *Canis,* in North America. When the first settlers started establishing settlements along the east coast there were no coyotes in those areas. There were some recordings of red wolves (*Canis Rufus*) in the Southeastern part of the country and grey wolves (*Canis lupus*) farther north. It was not until the early trappers of the late 17th century moved west of the Mississippi that coyotes, in numbers, were noticed and recorded. It has now been documented that coyotes have established populations in Maryland, Pennsylvania, New Jersey and other highly populated eastern states. There are many theories on why this has happened, but because of this eastward expansion of their range, hunting coyotes has gained in popularity.

The major difference between the subspecies of coyotes is size and color. Mid-western to western animals range in size from twenty to thirty-five pounds. A thirty pounder is a trophy. For the hunters in the eastern United States, thirty pounders are young animals. Some adult male eastern coyotes, grow to weights of more than sixty pounds. These individuals probably have some coyote-wolf hybrid genes.

Color also varies by locale. The area from eastern Montana, west to southeastern Oregon, to the crest of the Cascades is noted for pale creamy-colored coyotes. South and east, their color changes to a reddish brown pelage. There is also an abrupt change west of the Cascades in both Oregon and Washington and as far north as southern British Columbia. Animals there are dark brown to dark gray in color, and their fur is a great deal coarser.

Coyotes have seldom received much protection from humans other than radical animal rightists. With all the effort put into controlling these animals you would think their numbers would be held in check. From numerous studies conducted all over the Midwest and West, it has been established that the young of the year are the most vulnerable. Adult dogs, for the most part, survive from their early lessons. Young of the year average more than fifty percent mortality. An Idaho study in the late 1970s suggested that only about thirty percent of the adult population died during a year's time.

To become a successful coyote hunter year in and year out will take a little knowledge of their population density. Breeding season usually starts in late January in the southern part of their range and takes place during the mouth of February in most ranges. Friends from southern Alaska tell me that it is late March before their coyotes breed and July before the pups are visible. Gestation takes about sixty-three days. The hunter can use this to his advantage in hunting for animal damage control during the late spring and early summer. Usually there are three to five pups per litter.

Also diseases, such as distemper and canine hepatitis, have a bearing on local coyote populations, but the biggest single cause of mortality is humans. This mortality is not all

A coyote at full alert.

caused by small holes in the skin either. Trapping, snaring and the family auto all contribute to coyote mortality.

As I have already stated, *C. latrans* is no doubt the most adaptable critter in the United States. In fact, friends that live in the city limits of Los Angeles have videoed their "pet" coyotes raiding their garbage can. Everything was fine until Fido came up missing and a well-chewed hind leg from Fido was found behind the garage. Most coyotes that don't come in contact with people every day will establish a home range with as little a human distribution as possible. As litters are born and the young of those litters move into areas with higher human populations, the pups will become more humanized and lose fear of humans. There have now been documented attacks by coyote on humans and at least one death, a young boy in California.

Critters with relatively high rates of reproduction can withstand high mortality without hurting the general population. Most rodents fit into this category. With the exception of beavers, all rodents that live in North America mature within one year or less. The same holds true for coyotes. Although they do not have as many successful litters as the mature individuals, females of less than a year age do have litters. Also males that are less than a year old are sexually mature enough to fertilize females.

For years I have hunted the same areas and killed a high percentage of the coyotes that used those areas. The following year there seems to be the same number of 'yotes available as the year before. The only change I have seen is when there is an exceptionally high blacktail jack rabbit population. The coyote will increase the year after the rabbits have exploded. I'm guessing, but I think Mother Nature does her part with the coyote population too. When the rodent population is down, disease takes its toll and reproduction does not take place.

Right along with coyote populations goes the adage that top dog will be top dog. Adult males, and to a lesser extent females, establish a home range. Once you learn the home range of an adult male and kill that individual don't even waste your time hunting in that area for at least 30 days. There is no question that some pups of the year and the female will still be in the area, but knowing that the dominant male was killed will make them very cautious.

For western coyotes, home ranges vary widely. I've tracked individuals over eight miles in snow in a single direction. Females and pups seem to have a smaller home range.

Another important aspect for the successful hunter to know is the coyotes' feeding habits. Coyotes will eat anything. ANYTHING. Generally rodents make up the highest percentage of their diet. When rodents are not available, because of snow or just low populations, coyotes will attack and feed quite heavily on deer. When sheep are available coyotes seem to develop a taste for this kind of livestock. Livestock that die during the winter make excellent food for

This intense coyote knows something isn't quite right and is about ready to bolt. Note the animal's absolute concentration.

coyotes. Calling near these locations, even after the carcass has been totally consumed can be very productive. Coyotes have a habit of returning to a winter killed carcass long after all visible food is gone.

Studies have shown that during hard winters most coyotes will not spend the energy to kill big game, if carrion is available. When that food source is exhausted, deer become the mainstay of the coyote population.

During the winter of 1993-94, a very mild, easy winter, numerous coyote kills were sighted and documented in eastern Oregon. This leads me to believe that once an individual coyote has acquired a taste for deer, the deer are hunted in preference to other available food sources. When coyote control projects are carried out, there seems to be a direct

Here a coyote relaxes under good cover unaware that the hunter/photographer is nearby.

relationship with the increase of fawn survival in the area. The USF&WS has undertaken a study on the Hart Mountain Wildlife Refuge. After an Environmental Statement (EA) had been written and approved to hunt coyotes from the air, several radical preservation groups claimed that there were other factors affecting the fawn survival. The USF&WS undertook a two year study. In 1996, fifty-two antelope fawns were tagged in May. By July only eight of those fawns were still alive. The mortality was caused by a bobcat, one by a golden eagle and the rest by coyotes. In 1997, fifty-two more fawns were tagged and again by June 15 only eight were still alive. The question remains, will the refuge be managed for deer and antelope or will sound wildlife management buckle under to political pressure?

The last item of information that may be of some assistance to the coyote hunter is the behavior of both the adults and the young of the year. After mating in the late winter, both adults develop a den site. The den site can be anything from a dense thicket of evergreen blackberry bushes to holes dug in hillsides. The use of old homestead buildings that have fallen into their foundations as well as washed out tunnels in abundant irrigation ditches are common.

The male assists with the raising of the pups which offers a excellent chance to the beginning hunter to learn more about coyote habits. In late winter and early spring these breeding territories are defended. At this time just blowing on a rabbit distress call will not bring much response. Using a howler or mouth barks that sound like another dominant male will usually bring a quick response.

Other behavior that is of interest to the hunter is how coyotes communicate. Not only do they have a number of howls and barks, but their body posture is very communicative. The same behavior in domestic dogs can be seen. The young pups of the year will almost crawl up to a older male and lick his face in a very submissive manner. Two adult males that are aggressive will walk stiff legged up to each other. This type of manner will usually end in a fight. The same is true of coyotes in the wild.

The Use of a Howler

The use of a howler — there are many different kinds made — is a must for the complete coyote hunter. After pups start hunting on their own a "lonely coyote" howl will usually summon all the young of one family to your location in a hurry.

In the fall of the year, the use of a dying rabbit call will often bring the closest pups and maybe the adult. After hunters have killed off some pups of the year, those remaining become wary. Also, during the early fall most of the pups go off on their own to establish their own territory. As food is plentiful and rodent populations are at their highest, there is no need, other than companionship for the coyotes to be together. Hunting at this time of year usually draws singles, but don't completely discount it.

As the fall changes to winter coyotes pair up or even run in packs. This is the toughest time of year for the hunter, both two-legged and four-legged. Litter mates are now on the fur stretchers and the easy living of the early fall is gone. If the winter is hard and snow covers the ground, hunger can be serious. Rabbits that make up most of the fall diet of the coyote may be hard to obtain if they are even available. Hunting deer from the pack mentality is the surest form of 'yotes survival. The larger the pack the surer the chances of success. There used to be no way other than waiting out a fresh kill or using a howler to bring these coyotes into gun range. In the last few years the use of decoys and remote calls has solved the overly cautious coyote problem.

Coyotes are active all day long, but the most successful strategy is to use a howler to locate a coyote or family of coyotes just before dawn. Determine a half dozen different coyote locations before dawn and wait until it is light enough to shoot. The second best time is right at dusk. Quite often singles will howl just at dusk to group up for the night's hunt. At both these times they seem to respond to distress calls better than any other time of the day.

Now that you know all about what makes the Mr. Wily tick you can start planning your first hunt. If there is one thing I have learned in twenty-plus years of serious coyote hunting it is to expect the unexpected. Not only that, but expect them at the most unpredictable time. Details follow.

Cover Scent is probably the second most important thing you have going for you in the field. This is a two-part solution that, separately, is odorless. But when mixed together they produce a pungent skunk odor.

Chapter Two

RIFLES, SHOTGUNS
AND ALL THAT OTHER STUFF

If there is a type of hunter that has more gadgets than a coyote hunter, I don't know what kind of critter he is after. Since coyote hunting can be a year-round sport, clothing makes up a good bit of the investment. Within reason clothing is even more important than the firearm you may use. There will be a chapter devoted solely to camouflage and its use later in this volume.

For the longest time, I used to go to extremes to hide my body scent from coyotes. When activated charcoal Army Chemical Warfare suits became available to the public several of us tried them with good luck. The problem was they did not retain their effectiveness. Coyotes that six months before would swing into your wind path and come right on in to the decoy, would now turn and run as soon as they caught your odor. You will be able to tell this by the following actions: Coyote is circling you to be on your downwind side. All of a sudden the critter's nose will come up and he will be in high gear going the other direction. Mr. Wily just winded you. Since this happened, I have gone back to "Cover Scent" — the kind where you mix two solutions together, and the 200 yard scare stopped happening. Also, I got rid of the chemical warfare suit. The replacement was and still is what is known as "Shaggie".

Before going any further I must stress the single most important non purchased item in your whole coyote hunting resume. It is the ABSOLUTE REQUIREMENT THAT YOU REMAIN **STILL** once you get your rifle in your shooting sticks and your caller to your mouth or control box in your hand. The biggest problem any coyote hunter has is the distance from which a coyote can see the slightest movement. The single most important thing a good hunter has going for him is his ability to remain still as old wily looks things over.

When the coyote sees all is clear for him to come closer to the distress sound, he will usually come on in at a rather fast pace. These is where the squeaker becomes very

This hunter is wearing a full head mask. If you don't like getting your face dirty and don't wear glasses, this is the only way to go. The small portion of the light colored face probably will not be large enough for a coyote to see until his hunter is well past the stage of lighting the fire.

important. Not being a very good rifle shot, I need a standing target. I use shooting sticks 100% of the time, unless I am in the prone position. These sticks should be camouflaged too. With the shooting sticks, they can be positioned to provide a solid rest for your gun. There is also some leeway so the gun can be moved to get the coyote in the scope and still swing the gun with the moving target. Once the coyote is in the scope, push the squeaker once or twice. This will stop Mr. 'Yote immediately and he will look directly at you. Light the fire. The chances of Mr. Wily not picking you out now, even in your Shaggie, are slim. You will have up to four or five seconds to center your point of aim on the chest cavity and squeeze off the shot.

But, back to "all that other stuff".

There are many things, that will make your hunt more successful. Now we are thinking about the little things that so

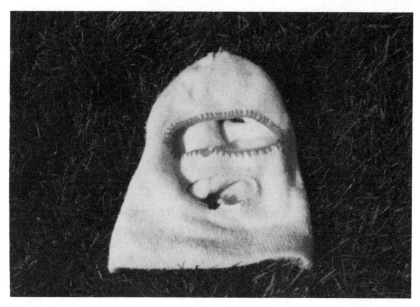

White ski mask to be used with snow camo suit or just white sheet.

often make the difference between success and failure.

Imagine that you have just driven up to one side of a two track that goes through a saddle between two low hills in a large piece of rolling sagebrush real estate. If you live in country that has tree cover or rolling tall grass then your approach may be slightly different. The main thing is to park your vehicle out of sight and walk into the wind if there is any.

If the road is like so many in the rural West, it may be used once a month. Park right in the middle. BEFORE you open the door, QUIETLY, make sure you have all the equipment you will need at the setup ready.

Different types of face coverings. Upper right: Full head cover. They are okay but cut down on side vision. Left: Camouflaged half mask. Excellent for hunters who don't wear glasses. Face will get warm in this type of camo rapidly and will lend toward fogging of glasses. Bottom: is a packet of face paint. Usually this is a combination of grey, black and brown. Coyotes are color blind, but the difference in shade and most of all the lack of reflection from the face is a must. For hunters who wear glasses this is about the only solution to face camo.

All the equipment is as follows:

•First, the caller. Take along at least one hand call, even if you are planning on using a electric caller. The electric has been known to go on the blink just after you have walked that half mile to that prefect setup.

•Knife, critter carrier, and vinyl seat cushion if there is snow on the ground or if the soil is fairly wet.

•Shooting sticks, bipod or something to rest your gun on while you wait for Old Wily.

•Rifle or shotgun and ammo.

Why have I left the firearms to last? They are probably the biggest area of disagreement. A great deal depends on your location. Having lived in the east, I see no need for anything larger than .22-.250, even for those sixty pounders. In fact,

This coyote is testing the wind for danger. The photographer is within 35 feet of this critter, using Shaggie as camouflage and cover scent to mask the human odor.

The Shaggie camo system is by far the best camouflage there is for any type of hunting. The key to this system is that it completely breaks up the outline of the hunter. There is no head, arm, shoulder, or body form to stand out for the coyote to see. Since coyotes are color blind it is not important that the colors blend exactly. Spring color Shaggies would work just as well in the fall as fall Shaggies work in the spring.

from conversations with friends that call coyotes in the East, or anywhere where there is fairly heavy cover, any rifle is my last choice. Even in the wide open spaces of the arid West a 12 gauge shotgun is the preferred weapon in the early season. If the cover is on the heavy side, my setup will have the likelihood of producing that critter at less than thirty yards. Many a time I have called wide open sagebrush basins were Mr. 'Yote should have come out of the stand of high sage in front of me, only to have the critter jump over the wire to the speaker at my left or right and be gone before I could get on him.

My first coyote was killed with a .22 pistol. It will also be my last. I want a great deal of skill involved from now on. If you do too, leave the .22 long rifle at home.

For the longest time I used a pre World War II Model 70, .22 K Hornet. It was a great little rifle, and it could drill coke bottle caps at a hundred yards on a regular basis. Some lucky

Another view of the Shaggie in use under field conditions.

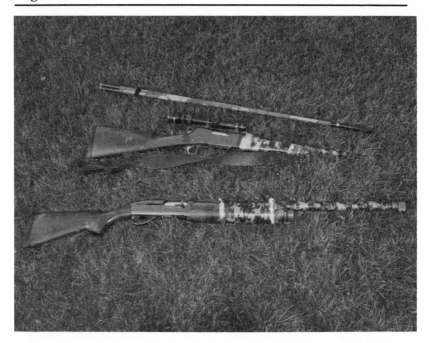

At the top of the photo is a set of camo shooting sticks. The left hand side of each stick is tipped with a hard plastic point that can be pushed in the ground. There are two Velcro strips that hold the sticks together so it can be used as a walking stick. When the set-up is reached the strips are undone and a single stick becomes a bipod. There is a rubber tubing on the end of the right hand side. This is to be used for the gun rest.

* * * * *

The rifle is a Browning BLR Remington .222. The barrel is wrapped in flat plastic camo tape down to the lower end of the forearm. The scope is a Tasco world class painted in flat black so there is little to no gloss or shine. The stock is finished with a flat oil finish.

* * * * *

The shotgun is a model 1100, finished in the same way, wrapped in camo tape. The reason for not wrapping the lower stock is it is more than likely behind a camo covered arm or next to a camo painted face that will pretty well break up the outline of the gun.

collector in the Midwest now owns it.

Coyotes are not hard to kill. They are thinned skin, have large lung area in comparison with other critters and require good shot placement, not brute force. Most notable coyote hunters like the .22-250. The case and design of the cartridge gives the hunter a great deal of latitude. For those long range shots it works fine. If you happen to call Old Wily into the more normal, less than a hundred-yard-shot and are loaded with a heavy load, you will kill him a great deal deader than he needs to be.

Also becoming popular is the .220 Swift, where long range shots are common. For those of us that place a great deal more importance on shot placement, the cartridge to use is the .222 or .223.

Since the little Model 70 departed and because I shoot lefthanded, I have gone to a Browning BLR .222. The loads are around 3,000 fps and I use nothing but 52 grain hollow

Squeaker taped to the left side of the front stock. If you shoot right-handed, it should be taped to the right-hand side of the front stock.

Critter carriers. These two carriers will help you keep the fleas off and will make the trip back to the truck a great deal easier. With the upper carrier, loop three legs through the loop and then bring the wooden handle back through the loop. Carry your coyote like a suitcase.

* * * * *

The second carrier is to be used to carry the critter over the shoulder. One front leg and one back leg are put through the cord loop and the weight of the coyote will snug the cord tight above the paw.

point bullets. The coyotes I have hit and lost I can count on one hand, and I am not that good a rifle shot either. My losses have been because of shot placement, usually in the abdominal area.

Low recoil rifles such as the smaller .22 center fires are by far the best fodder for coyote size animals. The 50 to 55 grain hollow point bullets are also preferred because of the lack of damage to the pelt. There is something magical about .22 bullets when they are loaded around 3,000 fps. They produce small entry holes and usually no exit holes. When the bullet misses a rib or other bones on the entry the exit hold is usually no greater than a fifty cent piece. It's best to hit a rib on the way in or some bone; seldom is there any exit hole.

The war stories about full metal jacket bullets would fill a library. I know of no sport hunters for coyotes who would recommend them.

Before going on with other equipment let me say one thing about scopes. On the Hornet was an old Weaver six power. This guy had all kinds of problems even getting fur in the glass. The BLR has a Leupold four power that is outfitted with a Premier Reticle. The Premier Reticle has a built in rangefinder. This way I can determine range and use the correct zero point. The Premier Reticle has three zero points. From experience, I've found out that the main reason for missed critters was the wrong judgement of range. The young of the year I would judge to be further than they were and the big old males I would think they would be closer than they actually were. With the Premier Reticle my zero points are 100, 225 and 300 yards. You can have more zero points if you have the gun to justify the expense.

Shotguns are also deadly on coyotes. Hunters who have access to 3½ inch 10 gauge guns can probably kill every coyote that comes within forty yards. My personal selection is a model 1100 with a polychoke. Most of the time I shoot the full choke and use nothing but 1½ ounces of copper plated BB's. The BB's will put any 'Yote in the dirt at 30 yards.

Copper plated BB's are harder to find all the time and with the increase use of steel shot handloading will become the only way to go in several years. If BB's are unavailable then go to the larger #4 buck and not smaller #2's.

The bottom line for most of you that desire to get into coyote hunting is you are going to use the firearm that you have available at the time. As soon as the "bug bites hard" give the above suggestions a hard look. For us old-timers, they have worked.

There are two things that are fairly important. One is

The author shown in his full length Shaggie camo system.

camo tape to fully cover that shiny gloss finish on most firearms. If you have chosen one with a camo finish forget the tape.

The other item that is important is a mouse squeaker. This is a small rubber ball with a metal reed in it that gives off a squeak when pushed. You will find many uses for this little item, the first being to stop that charging 'Yote so you can hit him where it counts. The second reason is to signal your hunting buddy, any of a number of prearranged signals, such as, you see something coming and he should get ready.

Other uses for the squeaker are to get that paranoid critter which is hanging up to come in a little closer so you can get a better shot. The first coyote I ever called and killed, was called the last twenty-five yards with the squeaker. The shot, to this day I still claim, was in self defense.

Finally, one piece of equipment mentioned under the list of needed items was a set of shooting sticks. These are made with three-quarter-inch pine dell sticks that you can pick up at any lumber yard. Camouflaged these with dull paint or, better yet, sew some camo cloth so they fit the sticks and glue them. Make them long enough to be used for walking sticks, if needed. The reason these are so important is because you must put the gun to your shoulder BEFORE YOU start calling. Remember the best thing going for Mr. 'Yote is his ability to see the slightest movement at great distances. The shooting sticks help me hold the gun to my shoulder while I wait for the coyote.

Locating coyotes in the pre-dawn with the use of a howler.

Chapter Three

PLANNING THE TRIP

Careful planning for your hunt starts at least the night before. It seems the best time to hunt is the latter part of the week when the critters have had a rest from all the "weekenders".

If you have a partner, the two of you will be very effective. That is, so long as that partner is still as a dead mouse and has eyes like an eagle. It does not hurt if he is a good shot too. There has been many a time I wished I had a partner to cover the back door.

If you are lucky enough to have another person who wants to learn coyote hunting like you, make sure you have similar interests. The same interest as you in a rewarding enjoyable experience. That does not mean that he is a great shot, but it does not hurt. A good coyote hunting partner is someone who won't bat an eye, even if a fly is in it. Or will not move an inch when brother 'Yote is standing out there at two hundred yards and acts like he wants to come closer.

How would your partner react to brother 'Yote jumping across his legs to get at that rabbit that is just about to give up the ghost, fifteen yards away? How patient is he at waiting out the best shot? If your partner likes to burn powder more than he likes to use his skinning knife, leave him at home. Coyote hunting partners require more patience than any other type of hunting I know. It requires that both partners have similar disciplines when it comes to show time. Companions must have the same likes and dislikes and interest in the hunt. I have found that if you can find three companions with the same temperaments and interest the coyotes are in for a bad time. The only potential problem is three times as much human odor out there, but eliminate that with cover scent.

One of things that I ALWAYS CHECK OUT THE NIGHT BEFORE is: weather. Hunting coyotes in wind over ten miles per hour is almost like hunting those pheasants in that asphalt parking lot.

Once assured there will not be any winds over ten miles per hour, consider what the other weather conditions are going to be, such as cloudy, partly sunny or full sun. Also, is there a weather front approaching? The best of all worlds would be

Sunshine in open country like this is nice, but high winds can play havoc with your coyote hunting. Check the weather when you plan a trip.

a cloudy day, with a cold front going to hit about sun up and no wind.

Your approach would be to drive the area you are going to hunt about a hour or so before it gets light enough to shoot. Stop the vehicle every half mile or so and listen for coyote talk. Listen for no more than five minutes at any one location. If you hear coyotes, make a mental note of the location. Move on three quarters of a mile or so and repeat the process. Don't wait for shooting light at that location. Usually the critters won't move out of hearing distance. Go find some more.

If you made five or so listening setups and hear no "coyote talk," start using your howler with the lonesome coyote call. If there is no response do not set up at that location that day. If there is a response, the next actions depend on how soon shooting light will be available. Where the coyotes are located and is the sun going to be at your back or shining in your face? Also, if there is a slight breeze is it in favor of the coyotes or in your favor?

If the wind is in your face, shooting light is ten minutes or less and the sun is to your back, look for the closest blind and sit it out. Otherwise the location becomes a setup for later in the morning.

Other factors to consider are: Do you know that there are animals in the area you plan to hunt? Have you seen or heard coyotes within the last few days? Do you know if anyone else has hunted the area in the last thirty days? In the early part of the season when you start hunting the ground is usually dry and dusty. Most of the West is in this condition, and day-old coyote tracks look just like week-old coyote tracks to most untrained eyes. Scat, poop, bowel movements — whatever you want to call it — is a better indicator of recent coyote activity in the area. If the scat is soft, smelly and shiny, load the gun, look for the nearest blind and do your thing. If the poop is hard and dull, keep moving. If it has started to turn white or grayish, head back to your rig and drive another mile.

After elk season, ask your elk hunting friends how many

coyotes they saw during their hunt. Also talk with game biologists after they have done their fall deer counts. Find out just how many coyotes they have seen and their location. These counts are usually done by plane and large areas are covered. This has been a real sure way of getting on some good concentrations in the late fall. There always seems to be some 'Yotes that have not been called or shot at when the deer first move to their wintering grounds.

If you are a big game hunter, you owe it to the resource to eliminate some of the predators that may prey on some of the young. The young just may be your target a few years from now. Plan a hunt for coyotes after the last big game season. The thrill of hunting will just be extended.

The reason I hunt coyotes, almost exclusively, is to have a rewarding and enjoyable time in the outdoors. But coyotes provide the biggest thrill, because of their intelligence and cunning. One of the most exciting experiences of a new season is that first over-zealous pup of the year that has to be squeaked to a halt at twenty yards, so you can shoot him. After a dozen or so of that kind of experience the thrill goes away and usually the easy kills too. By this time the coyotes and the hunter have gained a great deal of experience and respect for each other. If it was all easy, I would probably hunt ground squirrels in the spring and fish the rest of the year. If these critters were easy they probably have been extinct long ago. That's why careful planning is one of the main keys to continued success.

When I first started calling coyotes it was just drive out east of town, walk a few hundred yards off the county road, and I'd start playing the dying rabbit blues. Sometimes that worked, sometimes not, more than often — not.

Chapter Four

REMOTE CALLING

(**Author's Note:** *For those of you who happen have the first edition of this book, please notice that this chapter is not in your book.*)

Remote calling was just in the experimental stage when I was halfway finished writing the first edition of *"Coyote Hunting"*. Now remote calling has established its place in the sport. I know of few avid coyote hunters that do not think a remote unit is one of the most important items in their every day equipment. Just about every manufacturer of calling equipment makes a remote system. Some work great, others are so phony the coyotes are seen rolling in the dirt — laughing, I guess.

Even if you are a beginner and hunt with a partner you probably have done remote calling. A common setup is where you find a rolling hill landscape. The caller sets up in a location where he can see several hundred yards in a direction that a coyote probably would approach. Your partner heads for the next ridge on the downwind side. If this ridge is two or three hundred yards away that is just fine, you are the one that is going to be doing all the calling. If the time is early in the season and you are dealing with uneducated pups you will probably get the shot. If you are dealing with adults or are

A caller with a remote unit is a useful tool, one that most coyote hunters will find to be of great help in the field.

hunting later in the season your partner will get most of the shots. Coyotes learn quickly to use the wind to their advantage. My remote system has let me get forty to seventy yards away from speaker unit and I could get further if there was a reason. The control box will let me turn the caller off and on and turn volume up and down as the situation calls.

The way to set up is have the caller at a lower elevation than where you sit. Through trial and error, I've learned that the best location for the speaker is twenty to forty yards down from the skyline in a small basin. This is the ideal setup. If you have to setup on flat land then make sure your unit is hidden beside an opening that you can see well into the surrounding vegetation. You also must position yourself on a high location so you can see into that vegetation. This is the only reason I can see to be more than forty or fifty yards away from your unit.

Why such the concern for placing the unit BELOW YOUR SHOOTING POSITION? Most 'Yotes do not come to your call at full speed. Some pups, even in the fall, will want to check out what is disturbing that critter it hears. It may not be another coyote and he would not want to run over a 150 pound cougar, by accident. If your speaker is located below the surrounding skyline the incoming coyote will more than likely stop on the ridge line so he can see the location where the distress sound is coming from.

Expect three reactions when this happens. The first and most likely is he sees no big critter moving around where the sound is coming from and will continue toward the speaker. A decoy really helps in this situation. Second, if he sees a portion of the speaker and can not figure out what it is, he will sit down or lay down and watch the speaker. The coyote may stay in this position for as long as ten minutes. If this happens, light the fire. It is unlikely that he will come any closer. If you have not camouflaged your speaker and the coyote spots it right away, he will usually turn sideways to the direction he came from and stop and look back at the speaker. Light the fire in this situation too, as he is going to be leaving quickly.

From experience, I learned never place your speaker up off the ground. No more than a foot or so. Coyotes can pinpoint the location of the sound from a great distance. If the speaker is five feet up in a sagebrush it does have the ability to send the sound further, but that black thing that is emitting that distress sound is really out of place five feet up in a sagebrush bush. One time I called seven coyotes into a small basin. They all came in from a higher elevation than my set up. The speaker was located about five feet up in a bushy sage plant. This was very visible to all the critters that responded, but none came closer than seventy yards. My Remington 1100 just would not reach that far. Tough way to learn that lesson.

A simple little device like this, which plugs into the main caller and is called a "Louder," can almost double your calling range. This particular unit is manufactured by Johnny Stewart Wildlife Calls.

The reason remote calling is so effective is that it separates you from the sound that is attracting the predator. This gives you some, not much, but some leeway to SLOWLY MOVE, to get into position to make your shot. The coyote is concentrating on the speaker and the chances of him seeing you move is unlikely with the remote system. Decoys used with a remote system give the hunter even more of a chance to be successful. More on that later.

There are locations that many of us hunt that are so open, Wily can spot us at a half mile or further. In those locations, we usually look for some kind of cover that will allow us to hide and still see long distances. Remote callers work well in

This is an early morning photo of a coyote that came in the back door. The photographer had to move and shoot the picture at the same time. The reason for the bright golden eyes is a reflection of the flash. It shows just how close a coyote can be drawn into a decoy. The fawn is only 27 inches long.

these open spaces, but cover is low and hiding the unit is a problem. Manufacturers have come up with a new "other stuff" that solves that this wide open space problem. Calling critters that are out there over a mile away is near impossible under most situations. The new technology is an amplifier that will double the volume of the speaker you now have. In other words if you were considering upgrading your medium range caller to a long range caller let me suggest that you spend a extra ten bucks and get a "Louder". With the louder you can extend the speaker seventy feet from your control box. Seventy feet will allow you to hide in some good area and still see the coyote coming from a long ways.

If you have a long range speaker the louder set will easily call coyotes at a mile and a half. Just do not start off with this volume. Do nothing different, volume wise, until you have gone through your standard procedure. If you shot a critter and called for another five to seven minutes without a response, then turn on the louder and let her rip. (Suggestion) When using this piece of equipment, use ear plugs, as this thing can get loud enough to actually damage your hearing. Also do not run this call at top volume for more than ten seconds. If you are going to get a response, then Wily will be headed toward you in ten seconds or less. Wait at least two minutes before you go with the next series of calls and that series should be about half volume without the louder.

The louder cannot be used at the same time as the remote unit, but it seems to me that it is best to fit this system in this chapter. There is a way of stopping Mr. 'Yote away from you that will be discussed under decoys.

Chapter Five

CAMOUFLAGE AND DECOYS

If you are, or have been a successful turkey hunter, you are in luck. At least you know what camouflage clothing is all about. Bowhunters also have a feeling for what it takes to get up on either that royal elk or mossyback buck. Duck hunters sometimes use camo jackets for camouflaging their upper bodies in duck blinds. If you put all the keen scenes of the above animals into one critter you have the coyote. He has the eyes of a turkey, the nose that will make deer and elk take lessons, and the speed of a teal.

If you are a believer in the Bomengen ditch goose blind, you have already been introduced to the Shaggie. You just did not call it that. You probably first saw this outfit in the movie *Sniper*. In that movie the Shaggie was used to hide man from man. Hiding man from coyote is not that much different. Movement is still your biggest problem. The outline of a head, shoulder or arm is the giveaway. If you camouflage these body forms, you have pretty well made yourself a portion of the terrain to the coyote.

For the longest time I believed that the camo had to match the color surroundings. It does to a degree, but coyotes are color blind and as long as the outline of the hunter is well broken and remains STILL while the coyote is within sight, the hunter will probably be hidden. Coyotes have a hard time picking up the form of a hunter if the surrounding vegetation is higher than the hunter and the color pattern is fairly close to what he is wearing. For the longest time I would wear drab camo from head to toe. The head part is still very important as it is the most likely to be the part of the body the coyote will see first, especially the shine on your face. Soft camo hats with brims that can be pulled down partially over the neck are effective. The wider the brim, the better camouflage, but more interference with shooting. Soft baseball caps that can be molded to the head, so the Shaggie can cover them, are good, plus they are compatible in cold weather. I gave up on the camo boots but do stick to ones with dark colored soles. The rest of the outfit has stayed with me, even the face paint, if the cover I'm hunting in a particular area has a dark background.

When hunting in eastern Oregon's light colored soils or

This is a full-bodied rabbit decoy that stands about a foot high. When using this decoy it is best to have it out in an opening and your speaker hidden about five feet from the decoy.

when there are patches of snow on the ground, I can get away without face paint. Avid hunters usually use a face mask, which are great and sometimes a must. But we poor folks that wear glasses have missed too many easy shots because the lens were steamed up under a face mask to the point we could not see the critter until it was too late. Most coyote hunters prefer face paint to face masks.

This is a full bodied fawn decoy that is about 27 inches long and 22 inches high. The ears are detachable and you can roll the whole thing up and stick it in a fanny pack or hunting vest. It weighs about six ounces. This is the decoy to use when Old Wily gets dying rabbit call smart.

Folks who have the first edition of this book will remember how high I was on activated charcoal suits. No more. They worked great fresh out of the box. The problem was their effectiveness did not last. The charcoal absorbed odor to a point. I know of no way to reactivate the charcoal. Wily started picking up my odor at several hundred yards — and it was back to cover scent. The easiest to use is the kind that has two solutions that you mix together right on the spot. Once you are done with that particular hunting location, you can walk away from the odor.

Shaggie is a completely different concept in camouflage. The overcoat is made from very lightweight nylon webbing. To the webbing strips of burlap, green, brown and grey cotton and brown or grey light canvas have been sewn to the webbing. There is a hood that completely covers the sides of the hunter's

This coyote is about to take the bait — a plastic decoy. These decoys are very effective at holding the coyote's attention while the hunter slowly moves into shooting position.

face. The overcoat all of a sudden becomes part of the landscape. You put Shaggie on once you have arrived at the location you want to call. Please look at the adjacent picture, which was intentionally taken against a dark background so you can see Shaggie. If I had wanted to, I could have backed into a background where you could not be able to see me at all. The other nice thing about Shaggie is that it is light, less than two pounds, and can be carried either over the shoulder or suitcase fashion.

If you want to use Shaggie for other types of hunting where you move around slowly, you do not want the overcoat style. There is also a jacket and pants outfit made for archers.

The following photographs are examples of what Shaggie looks like as you would put it on and how well it breaks up your outline with a minimum of cover.

Excellent rolling sage-juniper country. Do you see the caller and coyote? Center front, but not very visible.

Several years ago I visited friends in Texas. They were coyote hunters and of course the discussion of hunting these critters came up rather quickly. Decoys have been used for coyote hunting for a long time. Some old-timers have trained small dogs to go out and have the coyote chase them back to the waiting hunter.

Another good decoy is a tanned coyote skin that you shape over PVC pipe to look like a live coyote. This idea was sent to me by a reader that lives in The Dalles, Oregon. I have never used this trick as it seemed more trouble than it was

Hunter dressed in Shaggie camo in a sitting position. Since coyotes are color blind this hunter, even though he is out in the open, is invisible to the prey. The rifle is the most visible item in the whole photo.

worth, but another coyote would make a good decoy.

My friends in Texas showed me a battery operated rabbit that moved backward and forward. This movement I'm sure would attract a coyote from several hundred yards. If used along with a call, the coyote would concentrate on the decoy until the hunter got a chance to get into shooting position. The only disadvantage was the weight. The rabbit by itself works fine. If placed out in an opening, close to the speaker, the coyote would have no problem picking it out.

This decoy had to be tried. While talking to the manufacturer of the battery operated rabbit I found out that he makes all kinds of decoys. One that seemed might be very effective for coyotes was a fawn. This polyform plastic fawn was light, slightly less than three feet long and easy to carry in a large coat pocket. It sets up on a collapsible rod and is full

Hunter rises to a shooting position. Notice that even in this stance, no arms, head or shoulders are visible.

bodied.

Since it was midwinter when I first got a chance to use the fawn decoy, I was packing a rifle instead of my camera. The rabbit tape, of course, would not do well with the fawn decoy. I had been using the fawn bleat since November. The two went well together. Using the fawn bleat also attracts deer. They run up to the caller, see what it is and leave.

Coyotes come into the caller readily, but when they don't see the fawn they usually will sit down and look at the hidden speaker. Soon they lose interest or go to coyote heaven. The problem is some will stop three or four hundred yards from my position. The decoy was the answer. Now they seldom stop other than to locate the fawn, which is in the open and within five to ten feet of the speaker.

I have not lost a fawn decoy yet, but as you can see from the photo they were less than five feet from the fawn when the flash from the camera went off. I have talked with hunters that have had rabbit decoys trashed by incoming coyotes. The hunter never saw them coming and old Wily got tricked when he bit into Br'er rabbit and there wasn't anything to it. A coyote quickly realizes that he's been had, but by then it is too late for the decoy.

Chapter Six

LOCATING MR. 'YOTE

There has been much written about using different calls. Again, if there aren't any pheasants in that asphalt parking lot, you aren't going to kill any. Learning to use a double reed call is fairly easy and if you purchase an electric caller, such as the Johnny Stewart M 512, the only skill involved is moving your finger. Well, it takes a little skill to know when to lower that volume and when not to play at all. The key now is, where do you find that critter?

The coyote has expanded its range to the point that it has populations in every state in the union, with the exception of Hawaii. The principles described in this chapter will hold even if you are hunting the palm meadows of the southeast, the wilds of northern Jersey or the remote high elevations of the West. The photographs used in this chapter were taken in eastern Oregon, but you should be able to adapt them, as a guide, to any location in the country.

Coyotes seem to have a pattern of approach to a caller's position, depending on where they were located. Their use of topography is by instinct. The ridges and draws may be barren in these photos, but if they were covered with blackjack oak in the South, beech and hickory in the North, or varying heights of grass in the Plains, the coyote would use them the same as it does in eastern Oregon.

Do not waste time just calling any place. Make sure there are coyotes in the area before setting up. The best way, of course, is to see the critters themselves. A responsible friend is another good clue if that friend knows what a coyote looks like. Newspaper reports of livestock kills that were not made by dogs would warrant a phone call to the farmer.

If you know there are a fair number of coyotes in the area you want to hunt, the process is a great deal easier. Drive the two tracks during the late summer and look for fresh droppings in the road. If there are cattle in the area that use large pastures, ask the rancher, if on private property, where his salt licks are located. The closer you get to the salt grounds the more definite the cattle paths will be, and the coyotes will use those paths.

Right after a rancher has moved his livestock out of one

Typical coyote country with barren ridges and sparsely-covered draws, clumps of dense sage and scattered junipers. An ideal place to locate the wily critters.

pasture, follow the fence lines with the most used paths and see if you can find fresh 'Yote tracks. It is really not to difficult to tell the difference between a single dog track and a single coyote track. Generally, dog tracks are more roundish than coyote tracks. The exterior toes of coyotes are larger than the interior toes. Dog's toes are of equal size. For me, there is a dead giveaway if I can follow a line of tracks in the dust or snow for some distance. Dog tracks tend to be offset. Coyote tracks are in a straight line when they are walking. The same goes for a fox, but the prints are smaller in size.

The droppings of coyotes are fairly easy to tell from dog scat. For the most part, the coyote droppings hold bone fragments of rodents and fur of the critters they have eaten. The segments are rapidly tapered at the ends. If the droppings are fresh and black in color, the coyotes have been eating

Here's a coyote moving right along the edge of a paved road in the desert country of the Southwest. Note the long-legged, lean build of this lanky coyote.

Trails like this that are well-worn into the earth by on-going cattle use in the area provide the coyote hunter an excellent place to set up. Here a hunter is moving into position to set up his electronic caller.

meat. Juniper berries in droppings are a dead giveaway that coyotes are in the area. I know of no dogs that eat juniper berries. In the East or Midwest I'm sure there is also some kind of berry that only coyotes will eat, usually in the winter, when other foods are scarce.

Another sure way of locating coyotes is to drive back country roads at dusk or a hour or so before sun up. During these two periods of time coyotes seem to be the most vocal. There is not anything else in the animal kingdom that sounds like a coyote. Wolves are a close second, but their range in the United States, even though it is expanding, is quite limited. Their howls are also deeper than the shrill song of the coyote.

Coyote footprint in dirt. Notice the print is longer than it is wide. Also the middle toes are are slightly larger than the outer toes. If it were possible to photograph you would be able to see that one foot is placed directly in front of the other, where a dog line of prints is offset.

Droppings are helpful signs of how fresh or old coyote activity in any given area is. For example, these droppings are very old — broken up and disintegrating. The critter was here about a year ago. If you find no fresher sign than this, keep moving.

This is a mixture of old droppings and some new stuff. With this much sign in the area, it wouldn't hurt to set up and call.

This is hot stuff. It's fresh, it shines, it's soft and it stinks. Coyotes are definitely in the area. Set up and give several calls in the immediate vicinity. Make your set-ups about a half-mile apart if possible.

This is old coyote droppings with sheep wool very visible. The hair of most critters that coyotes eat show up well in their droppings.

For the beginning coyote hunter this may be the stage in your hunting career that you should start learning to use the howler. There are many different models. They are made from everything from plastic to cow horns. All howlers are single reed calls. That means it is not just a blow-in-the-end affair like a double reed call. Howlers must have pressure applied to the reed in order to produce the desired sound. Locating coyotes, without the aim of killing, can be done in late summer and early fall with the aid of the howler. Try driving the dirt roads in remote areas and "blowing" on the howler. What you want to produce, at this time, is known as the lonesome coyote call. This is several short barks followed by a long howl. Instructional tapes are available with commercially sold

Magpies are one of the best indicators that coyotes are either on the way to your set-up or are already there. Here a magpie is looking at a well-hidden speaker in tall grass. This is shotgun country. If you see a coyote in this type of cover, it will be close.

howlers to give you a great deal better instruction than the above.

While you are mastering your howler you may get several different types of responses. A series of sharp "cow dog" type barks means you "blew it". It's what is known as the cow dog answer: A warning call to all other coyotes in the area that everything is not on the up and up. That's fine. At least you know there are coyotes in the area, and that is all you are trying to learn.

When you have mastered the lonesome coyote call, you get the same type of response back that you gave, several short barks and then a long howl or even two. If you are hunting and get this response, remain still, get ready and make sure the gun is loaded. That coyote WILL show. It may take a half hour if

Magpies follow coyotes into set-ups because quite often when a coyote makes a kill there will be something left for Mr. Magpie, especially if it is a deer.

Coyotes in the Southwest, from west Texas to Los Angeles on an east-west basis, and on up to central Colorado on a north-south basis, blend in very well to their surrounding vegetation. Here is a nice silver dog that blends with the dead, grey palm leaves and some native bunch grass in the California desert.

everything is not right, but he will at least take a look-see. If you are just out practicing or trying to locate coyotes move out of the area as quickly and as quietly as possible.

Those of you who bugle elk with a mouth diaphragm might try a series of high pitch barks or yips in a dime store plastic baseball bat. Cut the ends out of the bat and use it as a megaphone. The sound will reach a long way.

If you are hunting, miss a coyote and he is running away, one method to try to stop him is to give a series of injury-type yips on the howler. This injury-type yip will usually slow down, if not stop, the fleeing coyote. There are other ways of locating coyotes, such as winding up a fire siren, blowing a trumpet or making any series of high pitched sounds you can.

But, the howler has been the most positive way for most hunters.

One side item that will help any coyote hunter is the ability to know when a coyote is coming and from what direction. Those of us who hunt coyotes where there are magpies are lucky. For some reason when a magpie sees a coyote on the move he will either follow the coyote to the sound, more often, precede the coyote into the setup.

Sometimes coyotes will watch a magpie go into a setup to see how he acts. Magpies that show fear or flush wildly are a dead giveaway to the watching coyote. If the magpie settles down in a tree or sagebrush and just looks around, Mr. 'Yote will soon close in for a closer look.

For those of you who live in areas that have bluejays I understand that they will also investigate a woodpecker call. One key to remember is do not move or look at the birds. Birds seem to be able to pick up movement, just as well as the coyote, regardless how slight. Birds also are not color blind, where the coyote cannot see color as humans know it. If the birds are frightened away, there is little chance coyotes will come in.

The question I had for a great deal of time was WHERE should my setup be located? The first coyote I ever called on my own was from the very top of a long ridge in open sagebrush. I could see the world from up there. After setting up the speaker twenty feet away I put my butt into a big sage and proceeded to turn on the call. Wow, just like clock work about five hundred yards away, over the next ridge there came 'Yote — at a full gallop. I was set up with gun in shooting sticks, safety off and nothing but short grass for forty or fifty feet in front of me. Then the slope of the hill increased to the point that my next point of vision was about two hundred yards out on the draw bottom. The critter went out of sight at that two hundred yard point. After a longer-than-should-have-been wait, something moved to my left. There he was, twenty feet away with his nose almost all the way in the speaker. That

Excellent western coyote country with rims, rolling hills and open agricultural fields. When snow is in this type of country, drive the lower elevations (below) to see where and how coyotes are moving.

'Yote is probably still running. The point is, NEVER set up on top of a hill where you can not see at least fifty or more yards in all directions.

I still give that first area a try every year, but now the setup is about forty yards over the hill, about one-third the way down the slope. From this point I can see all but about twenty yards of draw bottom. I can't see past the top of the next ridge. I don't want to either. The four hundred yards of country now visible gives me lots of time to get ready.

The twenty yards of nonvisible area gives me time to quickly get into shooting position, while Mr. 'Yote is out of sight. When he reappears I'm ready to give him the squeaker and light the fire.

A few other don'ts are important for the beginner to learn. Rocks are a great place to set up. Usually you can park your butt well between two rocks and are solid when it comes to shooting. Coyotes have a difficult time seeing hunters in rocks and they are a likely place for cottontails to hide. One problem. Make sure that you have a good line of fire without any possibility of anything being hit by your fifty-two grainer. If you can set up at the bottom of the rock outcrop, fine. If you have to set up in the middle or top of the rocks, be aware of rocks that will interfere with your line of fire.

Once while trying to call a bobcat, I set up in rocks about two-thirds of the way up a rim. I expected the cat to come around the rim, and I had good lines of sight in both directions. What I was not counting on was a coyote coming off the hill across a major creek and straight up the slope to my dying rabbit. Not only did this critter come at full speed down the hill, but also up my side of the hill. There he was, fifteen yards in front of me, begging for that rabbit. The bullet just nicked a rock, about ten feet in front of the barrel. I was more surprised than the 'Yote.

Another time everything was set up right. Well hidden. Could see down the path through the broken rocks to the juniper hillside below. Turned on the caller. Bingo. There about one-half mile away, across a draw, the coyote started for me at a full run. He was so anxious to get that hurting cottontail that he even ran up the hill to the rocks. The problem was, I never checked out the line of sight in all directions. The shot was maybe twenty-five yards. I could see the upper portion of his white throat plainly in the scope. About five yards in front of me was a point of rock that obscured the critter's legs. Needless to say there was a slight puff of smoke in the scope when I squeezed the trigger. That coyote may still be running.

Another location that is great for seeing coyotes, but rough on getting them within rifle range is a large flat area with little to no cover that breaks up the skyline. Much of the

All of a sudden, there the coyote is — twenty yards away, looking right at you. Notice the high greasewood that the coyote used to get so close. In cover like this, you have to use a shotgun or the coyote will be gone as fast as it showed up.

country in the mid-Columbia Basin is flat, very flat. There are lots of song dogs in this area, but few locations to hide a hunter. There are a few areas that have large rocks; I mean VW size rocks. These are single rocks and well-scattered. They make great places to set up. Another good place to set up is where tumbleweeds bunch up for any reason. Many of the Midwest and plains states have large flat areas that have coyotes. There hunters prefer to set up in stream bottoms because of the cover to break up the hunters' outline. All that is needed is some brush that is higher than the hunter's head to break up his outline. For super fast action the stream bottoms are fine, but if the 'Yotes are the least bit paranoid they are going to be looking for you just as hard as you are looking for them.

The following is a series of photos that I hope you can adopt to your hunting country. Each photo has a "best setup" and an explanation why it is best. Also there is a description of how to get to the area. One question I've always had is, do you expose yourself to the skyline to get a better setup or do you stay hidden from critters and hope for the best? This is where experience is going to teach the beginner what to do when. Generally it is best not to cross a skyline. If you feel you have to cross a ridge, do it through a saddle or place where there is some cover.

Sequence of Coyote Coming In to a Call

Photos, in sequence from top left to right and bottom left to right, show: A. Coyote running toward hunter. After being called to the area with a remote fawn bleat. B. Coyote looking for fawn, but it only sees ground squirrels warning the neighborhood. Caller 30 yards to the right and now silent. Shaggie dressed cameraman using mouse squeaker to get coyote to come closer. C. Called coyote using a fawn bleat. Decoy CoverScent and remote caller. D. Coyote finally figuring out that distress sound was not coming from motionless decoy. Remote caller on the ground less than five feet from decoy.

Chapter Seven

CALLS AND HOWLERS

Predator calls have been around for a long time. I would not be surprised if some of the mountain men of the old West used their own voice to call some critters in, especially wolves.

Since the late '50's I have been exposed to these instruments. That is just what they are, instruments. Some callers have the ability to get a more realistic sound from their calls than others. It's an art for sure. Also, patience makes for fewer goofups when it counts. That is probably why I use an electric call most of the time.

Just because you use an electric call, though, doesn't mean you can just turn the thing on and let it play. There is skill involved in using this tool too. The first mistake most beginners make is to turn the volume to loud too soon. The only thing that does is send most critters fleeing in the other direction. Distress rabbit calls should start off at a very low volume. Some of my fastest action has been in high sage, shotgun terrain, within thirty seconds after I first turned on the call. The only time medium volume should be used is calling from the edge of an open grassy basin where you can see EVERYTHING for at least a half mile. Use full volume only after medium volume has been used for at least four minutes or longer. That usually means the softer volume calls have not produced any critters. If you use high volume, don't let it play

Occasionally you'll find that your calling will bring in other predators as well, such as this fine bobcat.

for over ten seconds. This is where the skill in using an electric caller comes into play. After the ten second blast, slowly start turning the volume of the call down.

If you pick up a coyote coming in, then play on his senses. Keep turning the volume down until it is very low and he is still coming. DON'T QUICKLY TURN THE VOLUME OFF WHEN YOU FIRST SEE HIM. If you can play that dying rabbit blues so you can hardly hear it and Mr. 'Yote is still several hundred yards away, but coming hard, get ready for the shot. He will usually come all the way into the speaker.

If the coyote is running hard or moving at a ground covering trot you can get away with moving your gun into shooting position. That is a sideways movement, not an up-to-your-shoulder movement. SLOWLY, move the muzzle of your gun to a location you believe the coyote will cross an opening. Pick one out fifty yards or so, between where he is and where he will be. If everything works right and he crosses the opening you have picked, give your squeaker one or two pushes. This squeak will usually put the brakes on Mr. Coyote and he will look directly at you. Be ready to shoot, as it is likely that he will be able to pick you out at this distance. The callers have done their job by this time. The rest is up to you.

Calls have been designed to imitate everything from mice to fawn deer. The most common calls produce sounds like that of a rabbit in distress. For hunters in the East the cottontail rabbit is the most used. If there are jackrabbits, both black tail and white tail, a jackrabbit call will produce.

Other calls that have produced for hunters are woodpecker, fox pup or coyote pup distress calls, and even housecat kitten screams. For the last several years in my area the fawn bleat has worked year around. Few other hunters are using it and coyotes seem to have little suspicion of the sound.

All the above calls are also available on cassette tapes. There are a number of quality producers of battery operated cassette tape players. The development of cassette players improved during the 1960s and 70's. My good friend Ray

Johnson purchased a Johnny Stewart cassette player in the mid 70's. This player was operated by twelve 1.5 volt "D" batteries. It worked well and many hundreds of coyotes have bitten the dust from the sounds this caller has put out. My first cassette caller was the same 1.5 volt battery affair and it is still working. There was only one problem with this caller — the weight. Just the speaker is close to seven pounds. I'm not sure what the whole affair weighed, but if I drop more than one coyote at a setup I have to make two trips to get all my equipment and the coyotes back to the truck.

Today's cassette callers weigh less than seven pounds and produce better quality sound than the old 1.5 volt battery type did. The big advantage to today's cassette players is that are rechargeable and can play up to fifteen hours without being recharged. They can be plugged into a cigarette lighter or a standard 110 outlet to recharge. The biggest advantage they give the new hunter is the capability to continue to call without any movement. This is something the handheld calls cannot do.

Different types of caller tapes and instructional tapes.

The sounds from these callers are so realistic that I've seen coyote pups literally put their noses right in the speaker, looking for that wounded rabbit.

There is a great deal of difference in price between a several hundred dollar cassette player and a handheld call which costs less than ten dollars. For the beginner, the handheld call will be the best to start with. In the early season with a bunch of uneducated pups of the year a handheld call will do fine. If there are many coyotes around and the beginner is successful at bagging a few, the bug will have bitten and a cassette player will be on the top of the list for Christmas.

Every coyote hunter should have several different calls. At least one single reed call, one double reed call and the howler. The single reed call will usually produce the best quality of sound. Mouth calls have a disadvantage in that they

A variety of calls are available to assist the coyote hunter, including mouth diaphrams with great range and diversity of sound potential from a number of manufacturers, plus out-of-the-mouth tube or squeaker calls.

are hard to clean and they get out of adjustment easily. Double reeded calls are fairly dependable. They produce a reasonably good sound and when that battery in the cassette player gives up, just as you see brother 'Yote look over the hill, the double reed call can take over.

The howler is a single reed affair that reproduces the sounds of the coyote. There are a number of brands, and all can produce a number of sounds. These include the forementioned lonesome coyote call, which is the one most used to draw coyotes to your location. The distress pup yip, will usually stop any coyote. The warning bark is only used when you want to scare everything in the county out of the country. The dominant male bark can be just as well made with the human voice box as blown on the howler. This bark is used in the spring when you know there is a den close by

Close-up of rodent squeakers. These are used to call in close hiding coyotes or to stop a charging coyote coming at you full speed. They will usually come to a stop if they hear that high pitched squeak. That gives you a chance for a standing shot.

and you wish to get the male to expose himself.

One other call, also previously mentioned, but important enough to mention again, is the rodent squeaker or coaxer call. This call does not have much range, but is extremely effective in getting coyotes to come closer for a better look. Tape one to your rifle or shotgun, on the fore stock. More often than not you will use this call to STOP the charging coyote. The reason they stop is because the sound is different and coming from a different location. If you shoot left-handed, tape the squeaker to the left-and side of the fore stock.

Plastic Howler — This is the best howler for all weather and for best quality sound. This is a single reed howler with a cover for protection. This tool is not only for locating coyotes, but also for calling them to the hunter. It works well in the early fall when family groups are beginning to scatter. The pups will come to the lonesome call. It also works well in winter after a season of dying rabbit blues has worn out its welcome.

This coyote came in fast and is just about ready to leave as fast. You can tell it came a long way because its tongue is hanging out. Coyotes can hear electric callers and will come to them from as far away as a mile.

Chapter Eight

WHERE TO SET UP
AND WHERE NOT TO WASTE YOUR TIME

We are just about ready to start the final phase of putting that first 'Yote in the dirt. Once again the number one rule is not to move once you are set up — for any reason other than life or death.

Knowing the country is a very big plus and most of us who have been at this game have our favorite setups and know the most effective way to get there.

One of mine is less than five miles from beautiful downtown Baker City. It's about fifty yards off a seldom used county road. High sage gives me a blind for my truck and a short walk to a rather steep draw is covered quickly. There is one large sagebrush bush that is used for a blind. It is located just under the crest of the hill so I can see a 100 percent of what moves up or down the draw. Across the draw, three hundred yards or so is the beginning of a large sage flat that is close to a half mile wide. The elevation of this flat is slightly above the elevation of my setup. The reason this is good is that it is very unlikely that any coyote will see or hear me move from the truck to my setup. If he sees me there is a very good chance I will see him. I have the choice at that time to take a shot or try for another one that has not seen me. If I can stop the fleeing 'Yote with a few squeaks from the coaxer, I'll take the shot. If he is in high gear and shows no interest in slowing down, I won't shoot.

The whole area is covered by fairly high sage. Plants that are three to four feet high gives the approaching coyote some security. It's great for the hunter too, because the setup is so high on the slope that the critter can't move, even in the high sage without me seeing him. I know coyotes use this area all year long and this setup has never failed me on a yearly basis, especially since it is only called once in the early fall and once about Christmas time.

To break down the superiority of this location over others will give the beginning hunter things to look for and some to forget.

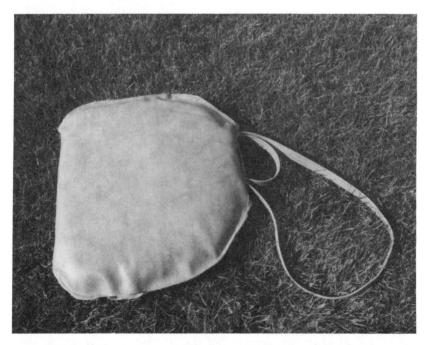

Vinyl covered seat for sitting on snow or wet ground. The two handles are for either carrying it in your hand or slinging it over your shoulder. A must when you're hunting in wet or thawing snow.

1. Is there a good place to hide your vehicle so it can't be seen? Even though coyotes are used to seeing all kinds of rigs they know which have been sitting out in the brush for a while and which have just arrived. Coyotes that end up on my stretchers have had to see my truck on their way into the setup, but I've also watched in horror as a fully charging coyote came to a abrupt stop, turned sideways, looked directly at the visible truck, and departed a great deal faster than he approached.

2. The distance from the truck to the setup is short. This means that it is not very likely that the hunter will expose himself to a coyote that is close by. In this way, sound from walking in and setting up is kept to a minimum. If you are

A well-hidden hunter in the shadow of a small juniper, all set up for a coyote to show up. Notice that the speaker is right beside the hunter. If there is no place to hide the speaker fifty or so feet away, this will have to do. Notice that the rifle is to the shoulder, resting on the shooting sticks, which are also camouflaged.

Set-up on top of ridge. Bad location, can't see coyote for over 100 yards. When you do get to see the coyote, it is too close.

Same location, just twenty-five yards further DOWN HILL. Can see coyote approach much better and keep it in sight for several hundred yards. Good set-up.

using a mouth call the chances of being seen are a great deal more, than if you are using a electric call.

The biggest advantage is the separation between the speaker and the hunter. If a coyote is circling your position to get down wind he may take a route where he can see the area where the noise is being made. If the speaker is well-hidden fifty or sixty feet from the caller, then it is unlikely that the hunter will be spotted. The further the speaker is from the hunter the better. With remote control the best distance is thirty to forty yards.

Most cassette callers come with a twenty foot cord. This is probably more than enough. I have added an additional fifty feet to my M512. It is a hassle winding all that wire up at every setup, but it sure pays off in the number of coyotes on the drying boards every year. I've even had those furry critters pass closer than twenty feet to get at the speaker fifty feet away.

While on placement of the speaker it may be important to discuss location of the speaker. Place it in a dense piece of brush or hide it slightly between two rocks, something that will break up the smooth round configuration. Hunters who use electric callers have found if they can get the speaker a foot or so off the ground, the sound seems to carry further with better quality.

Once again I would like to remind you of the time I called in seven coyotes. The reason for not getting any to come within shotgun range was the speaker was located five feet off the ground and was very visible to the coyotes that approached. The speaker was placed rather high in a bitter brush plant, not so visible to the critters that were going to come up the draw but very visible for those coming over or around the hill. Needless to say the fire was never lit. The 'Yotes came to within seventy yards, eyed the speaker and wandered away. None of them acted afraid, but none wanted to come any closer either.

If you must set up in some low vegetation, find some

rocks to break up the speaker outline. It is very important that the rocks be higher than the speaker. To find a location that has both a good hunter setup and a good speaker setup within fifty or sixty feet of each other is unusual. In most cases like this the hunter location is the most important. The speaker usually can be hidden off the ground a few inches and within some kind of cover.

There are some photos to follow that were taken in eastern Oregon, but the principles that I give as tips will be helpful from the flat lands of Kansas, to the pine barrens of southern New Jersey, to the steep canyons of the Rockies and the Far West. There are also some photos of places NOT to setup. Each photo has a explanation with that photo and locations are marked on the photo.

The adage that you should never say never sure applies to coyote hunting. No doubt I will receive some letters from new hunters who say they just piled up the critters right in a spot where I suggested they not set up. I follow my own advice and every year I still get my adrenalin kicked into overdrive by some 'Yote jumping over the speaker cord to get at that dying rabbit, from a direction I just knew he should not come. That's why I still am hunting song dogs and not other kinds of less intelligent critters.

PHOTOS OF SET-UP SITUATIONS
YOU'LL ENCOUNTER IN THE FIELD FOLLOW

This photo is looking to the west in the early morning. (Sun to your back if possible.) Junipers are large, but scattered, not much ground cover. Once coyote exposes itself, you can wait until it stops between junipers. Open ridges on far side will have to be crossed to get a closer look at the rabbit that is in a world of hurt. Broken rocks in foreground with grass make an excellent location to set up, but there are many side draws the coyote could come up.

* * * * *

Enter area from right hand side of ridge and move into set-up area from shadow of juniper. Find a saddle to cross the ridge. Do not expose yourself on the skyline.

Here is an excellent set-up for coyotes. There are open ridges, deep brushy draws, little ground cover and the deer have browsed some of the junipers so the ground is fairly open. An excellent "blind" would be to sit in front of the small juniper on the right side of the photo, facing the draw, downhill.

Large mostly flat area with very tall sagebrush. Photo is taken from a slight rise so you can look into the sage and see the opening. This is an excellent location for a set-up as there is fairly thick brush on the rise and open shooting lanes for at least 180 degrees. Also, there are several brushy draws within a half mile that could harbor several coyotes. Old road through the middle of the photo would be the most likely approach.

Examples of large flats, great for seeing coyotes, but very difficult to hide so you can break up your outline. Not a good place to set up.

Typical rolling hills, grass and sagebrush country. The high sage in the foreground of the picture would make an excellent location to set up and call. Any coyote coming over the hill, around the hill or down the draw would make an easy target.

Beautiful country but a setup at this point doesn't give you a good view if a coyote should come in. Locate a better spot.

Here a setup in high sagebrush allowed the caller to bring this coytoe into shooting range.

Ideal set-up in typical western coyote country. If you live in the East or Midwest, just replace the sagebrush with trees. Notice the hunter is set up on a slight rise with the sagebrush slightly higher than his head. The only really visible portion of this hunter is a portion of his hat and the scope on the rifle. This hunter can cover about 120 degrees of hillside and draw bottom without moving too much. His field of fire is excellent and if you look real closely you can see the caller speaker very visible midway up a large sage plant in the right center portion of the photograph.

This photo is taken in eastern Oregon, but could be anyplace in the Plains states. Dark objects are rocks that are almost VW size. They need not be rocks, but could be low brush or large clumps of grass. Even though this looks as if it would be difficult to call, it is not. Set the speaker away from the rocks in the grass and with the use of a decoy this setup should be one of your best bets. Getting to the setup without the coyote seeing you would be the toughest part. You should be able to see Mr. Wily coming from a long way.

This hunter is well hidden from an approaching coyote. The important thing here is that the outline of head and shoulders of the hunter are broken up by the tall rabbit brush behind. Again shooting sticks are used. This hunter is expecting the approaching coyote to come up the draw out of some tall sage. If the coyote comes over the hill behind the hunter, he will have to wait until the coyote is in the tall grass in the background and then and only then SLOWLY MOVE to a better shooting position. If the coyote is moving in tall cover and the hunter can see it moving, it is okay for the hunter to move, but only when the coyote moves.

Well camouflaged hunter hiding in tall grass with an unseen pond behind him. There will be no back-door surprises using this type of set-up. The shooting sticks show this hunter is expecting to have the coyote come around the hill in the background or along some high sage out of the photograph.

Chapter Nine

NOW THAT YOU GOT HIM, WHAT NEXT?

There lies the prettiest coyote you ever saw, your first. Now what do you do with him? More prime, high grade coyote hides are ruined by poor pelt handling than by using Grandpa's moose gun on the critter.

Let's assume that you have followed all the instructions in the preceding chapters and have a clean kill, little, to no blood showing. The pelt should be removed as soon as possible.

In the early fall fur can be ruined in just a few hours. If the weather is warm and the bullet has penetrated the intestinal cavity, I notice fur slippage can happen in less than two hours. Skin your critters just as fast as possible and don't wait until you get them home.

The other extreme is cold weather. The animal will not suffer any fur slippage, but skinning frozen coyotes is just plain work, slow hard work.

Partners accuse me of skinning the critters alive. I do start immediately, after reaching my truck. (Enclosed are several photos of the setup I use to hang and skin coyotes) The setup shown is not my invention. To the best of my knowledge, Ray Johnson, of Lakeview, Oregon, came up with this appendage to a rear bumper. It has several advantages over

The easy way of getting your critter back to the skinning area is with a coyote carrier. There are two types. One you carry like a suitcase and the other over your shoulder. With either type, you place the nylon rope through O-rings, which allow the rope to slip right above the critter's dew claw.

other gambrel hanging methods. First, everything can be carried right in the truck. The base is a piece of one-half inch plate steel. Welded to this plate is a inch piece of two inch, threaded steel pipe. The base plate is welded to the truck bumper. The base plate is seven inches wide at the truck end and five inches wide at the end facing away from the truck. Two and one half inches of the plate are welded to the bumper. Corners are rounded. The two inch pipe is centered four inches from the wide end of the plate. There is a 4½ inch by 1 3/4 inch pipe screwed into the two inch pipe. That pipe should not be welded. It should be well oiled so it can be removed for cleaning during the season. About twice a season dirt will build up inside the 1 3/4 inch pipe so the gambrel hanger cannot fit inside the 1 3/4 inch pipe. My gambrel hanger is 1½ inch diameter steel pipe, 54 inches long. Individuals will want to custom-make this apparatus depending on their height and skinning comfort levels. At the end of the gambrel hanger is a one-half inch piece of cold, rolled steel rod, welded to the 1½ to 2 inch pipe. The steel rod is to hold the gambrel and is welded so the open end of the "U" is facing upwards.

I use a nine inch wide gambrel, but any reasonably wide gambrel will work on coyotes as usually only one leg is skinned at a time and the other leg is left hanging so it is out of the way.

The only time I ever DO NOT SKIN my coyotes "right away" is when they are shot in the head area or lower neck, thus creating a great deal of blood. Rarely, coyotes are shot on an especially rainy day and they seem to get covered in mud. When this happens they take their last bath in the closest creek. Skinning bloody or muddy coyotes really make the fleshing job a great deal more difficult.

The method that is shown is called the cased method. Coyotes are always sold cased with the fur out. As you skin the coyote the fur is rolled under the pelt that is still attached. The nose is the last to be cut off and this is the way the pelt will be fleshed, but not for transportation back to the fur shed.

Start your first cut just below the back leg elbow. Take care not to cut the any of the major tendons. Start with a cut straight down the inside of the back leg where the brown fur meets the lighter colored fur. Cut all the way to and around the anus. Repeat the same process on the other leg. Once the skin is cut above the leg joint the skin can be pulled and worked all the way to the base of the tail. Sometimes the skin on the upper part of the back leg is difficult to remove without cutting. In these cases look carefully for a whitish-pink membrane. If at all possible leave this membrane on the body. The tail bone can either be left on the body or cut off and removed when the animal is fleshed. At this time start looking for the tail end of the saddle muscle. It starts right in front of the hind legs. Beginners can cut as little of this muscle as possible without damaging the pelt. Leaving this muscle on the body will become easier after skinning a few animals. Pull the

Nice pale, eastern Oregon coyote with all the tools needed to turn it into an excellent pelt. The rubber gloves are a must. The steel or other sharpening device is to keep your knives sharp.

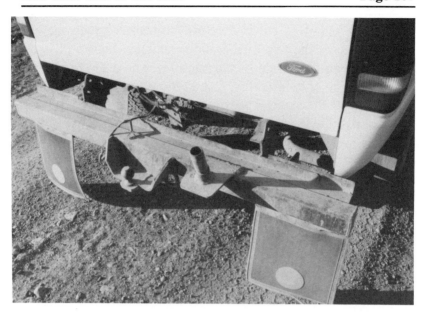

Truck tools for skinning coyotes. Half-inch steel plate welded to bumper. Two-inch threaded pipe welded to plate.

One and three-quarter inch pipe placed inside welded pipe with welded steel rod to pipe. The steel rod holds the gambrel.

Nine-inch-wide gambrel is best for coyotes.

Photo shows the gambrel in place, ready for use.

hide all the way to the back side of the front legs. This area is the most difficult area on the coyote to skin. It is a area that you will have to learn by experience. A suggestion would be to leave as much fat and meat as possible in this area so you do not cut the pelt. Pull the skin up over the base of the ears. Cut the ears so the opening is no larger than a inch to a inch and one half in diameter. Care is needed cutting around the eyes. Leave as much of the eye lid as possible. Small eye lid holes make the pelt that much better looking. Skin the lower jaw at least half way down to the end of the muzzle. I find it more attractive to fur buyers to cut about half the fur on the lower jaw off at this time. Skin out the upper muzzle to the nose and remove the nose with the pelt.

Immediately after skinning, turn the pelt right side out. This way the leather will not dry out and will stay relatively clean.

Fleshing is the process of removing all fat, meat and gristle from the skin, properly called the leather. It is a very difficult process to describe in words much less pictures. Before fleshing can start all burrs and other foreign objects must be removed from the fur. If they are not, it is very likely that they will cut a hole, some of major size, during the fleshing process. A steel Poodle comb will do an excellent job on all caked mud, dried blood and small "stick'ms". Large cockle burrs present another problem. My best success has been to carefully pull a few of the guard hairs away from the burr at a time. Once you get started the process becomes easier and finally the burr can be separated from the remaining guard hairs with ease.

Next you need a fleshing board. This is a hardwood board, with no knots, about five feet long. The top part of the board should be about 1½ inches wide, not a point, and about seven-eighths of an inch thick. The fleshing side of the board should be beveled and sanded smooth. Within fourteen inches of the top the board should widen to seven and one half inches and hold that width.

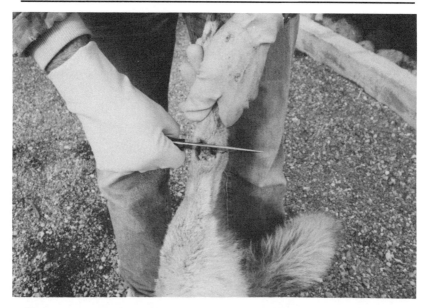

First cut, just below the back leg elbow. Take care not to cut any tendons.

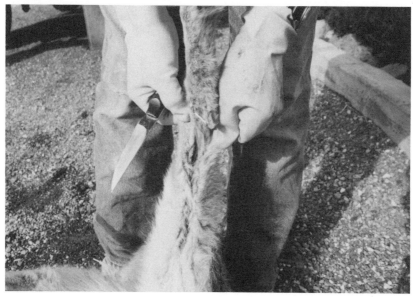

Cut straight down the inside of the back leg where the brown fur meets the white fur.

Work the back leg skin all the way to the base of the tail. About half of this work will be knife work. The other half is slow, steady pulling.

The best way to learn how to flesh an animal is watch someone else do the job. If you know no one, then you will have to teach yourself. It is an art that you must learn by doing. Fleshing knives for coyotes are two handle affairs. They are similar to draw knives, but have an inner, concave, rounded fleshing side and an outer, convex cutting side. The fleshing side has a dull rolled-over edge that is used on almost the complete hide. The other side is sharp, and is ONLY USED for the toughest, grisly part around the ears. On all my coyotes, except the oldest males, I use the rounded blade to flesh the whole animal. As you make mistakes in the process, you will learn that an easy even pressure will gain the best results.

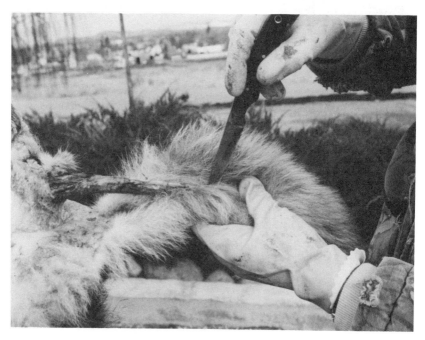

The tail can be skinned at this point or left for later. This photo shows the tail skinning process, but more importantly shows the very end of the whitish-pink membrane that is the end of the saddle muscle.

Coyote with saddle muscle remaining on animal. Makes the fleshing job a great deal easier. From finishing the skinning of the tail to this point is all pulling — no knife work once the saddle muscle is secure to the leg area.

In order to keep the fleshing job as easy as possible, work up to "clean skinning" your animal in the field. Do not try clean skinning at first. Just learn how to get the hide off the critter without too many cuts in the pelt. As you learn the coyote anatomy you will learn where you can use your knife and where you must gently pull the hide from the body with your fingers. One area of extreme caution is the inside of the front legs.

Once you have skinned out the hind legs and tail area, the hide can be pulled all the way to the back side of the front legs. From there, until you have freed the front leg skin below the elbow, requires a careful skinning job. Beginners, do not be afraid to leave a good bit of fat and even meat between the front legs and the lower throat area. This is a great deal easier to remove with a fleshing knife than trying to skin clean.

Photo shows saddle muscle better, but the tail has been cut off for later skinning.

Pull the hide all the way to the back side of the front legs.

Gently cut front leg area. Don't worry about leaving meat and fat on this area of the pelt. It is one of the hardest to skin, but easiest to flesh.

Another method to deal with the skinning of the front legs is to use your gloved fingers to work the skin away from the upper leg. This is tough work, but does the cleanest job.

This front leg opening is used to hold the pelt in place during the fleshing of that half of the pelt. The process is repeated for the other half. Sometimes it is best to trim the fat around the tail with a sharp shinning knife rather than to try to remove it with the fleshing tool. Then move the hide so the ear openings hold the pelt in place and repeat the same process from the area around the ears to the front of the shoulders. All fat, muscle and gristle must be removed so the pelt can dry quickly.

The fleshing job becomes easier as the fat layer between this muscle and the skin is exposed. Coyotes really are not difficult animals to take care of once you learn the how to's.

After the hide is fleshed you will need to dry the pelt. This is a two step process. The first step is to turn the pelt, FUR SIDE IN, and let the excess moisture evaporate from the leather. Once the leather side of the pelt feels dry to touch, turn the pelt fur side out and replace the pelt on the stretcher.

At this time it is important to center the pelt for final drying. This means the eyes and ears are equal distance from the side of the frame and the center line of the back is straight and centered.

Several different kinds of drying frames are used to dry coyote pelts: solid wood, wire and adjustable wood. The adjustable wood is by far the best. Not only is it capable of handling mature animals as well as the young of the year, but it dries the pelts quicker because of better air circulation.

The stretchers that I use are made of better grades of ponderosa pine, few tight knots and straight grain. It is important that the wood hold a push pin well, not split and absorb slight amounts of moisture if a hide is still damp when turned. Basically stretchers are six feet long, sawed down the middle and hinged at the top. The sides are beveled. Starting at the top they are round and slope from less than a inch wide

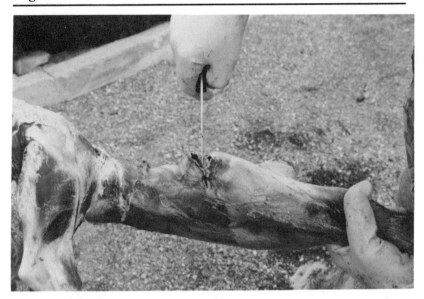

Pull pelt over the base of the ears and cut ears so the hole is no longer than 1½ inches in diameter.

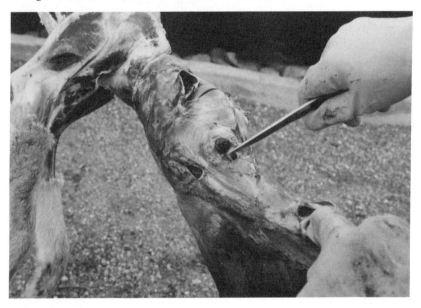

Care is used in cutting around the eyes. Leave as much eyelid as possible.

at the top to about 6½ inches wide, 14 inches from the top. From this point, they widen to 10 inches at the base. There is a adjustable slide at 62 inch mark (most coyotes' tail tips will reach this mark). This enables me to spread my hide and not have it bag on the frame. The crosspiece of wood is held in place by two lock wing nuts, one on each side of the frame. For hunters in the East or Midwest, who have access to linden or basswood, I would recommend these woods in place of ponderosa pine. Also the above measurements will have to be increased to handle the larger animals.

Now that we have gone all through the work to find, call, kill, skin, flesh and dry the coyote, we either want to have it tanned and hang it on the wall or sell it. Fur is not like most other commodities. If there is a cold winter, heating oil goes up on the commodities exchange by the minute. Fur is completely dependent on a few fashion designers who work in

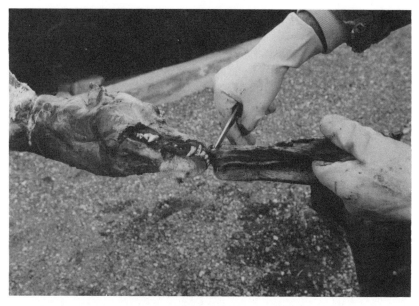

Skin the lower jaw at least half way down, then cut, leaving about half the skin on the lower jaw. Keep skinning to the nose and cut the nose so it remains with the rest of the pelt.

The pelt will be inside-out. Do not leave it this way during transportation. Turn it fur side out until you are back at the fleshing board.

Europe and New York. Asia is becoming more of a fur fashion center the last few years, but that market is for specific animals.

Coyotes are mostly used for trim on expensive winter clothing such as ski parkas. During the late 1970's and early '80's, coyote coats were very fashionable. Some select coyote hides were selling for as high as $100. By 1988 demand was so low that a good eastern Oregon coyote was selling for $12. The money that can be made from coyote hunting is not a reason to hunt. You will be lucky if you can pay for your gas.

Since the animal rights movement started some folks have decided that it is just not worth the hassle to wear visible fur, thus the demand has remained low into the mid '90's. Early in 1994 there was a definite increase in demand for coyote pelts, so it may be safe to say that this product is coming back, but don't count on it.

The best way to sell your pelts is through state fur sales. There are several advantages to selling this way.

First, you have the opportunity to see other hunters products. See how they take care of their fur. This way you can pick up ideas to improve the handling of your own pelts.

Second, you have the right to place a price on your pelts. There usually are ten to twenty buyers at these sales and they must compete against each other in order to fill their outstanding orders. If your price is not met by one of the buyers you do not have to sell. If the asking price is met the sale is closed.

Third, you meet other hunters and there is always talk of new products and some little special technique that works under some special condition.

State sales are held starting in late December and throughout the winter until late March. It is usually best to sell your pelts early in December or January. This is not always the case, but in more years than not this scenario will hold true.

After the fleshing job the leather should look white. Place the fleshed pelt on the stretcher skin side out until it is dry to touch. At this time turn the pelt so it is fur side out for the rest of the drying process. When the nose is hard, the pelt is dry cured and is ready for tanning or sale.

* * * * * *

A fan helps the drying process. Not only does it move the moist air away from the skin, but also fluffs the fur.

One last thought on coyote hunting. Regardless of how good hunting is, you are out there for the sport and the enjoyment of the outdoors. Learn from this book and pass the sport on to your children, grandchildren or the kid down the block. See you in the sage.

The author with a coyote taken using techniques described in this book.

Chapter Ten

AND THEN THERE ARE THE SURPRISES!

With thirty-plus years of chasing coyotes it would be safe to say that there have been a few surprises over that period of time. Any beginning hunter should expect these. Needless to say, they get the adrenalin pumping and they sure add to the excitement of the hunt.

The best way to describe what to expect is to relate some personal experiences that have taken place in recent years.

For most of us who hunt coyotes, bobcats are also part of the ecosystem. They coexist with coyotes in many of the same habitats nationwide. Some regions of the country have sufficiently strong bobcat populations where the intentional calling of bobcats is fairly easy. In most locations, however, bobcat populations are low just because of the type of prey available and the bobcat's reproductive capability.

Most coyotes will come into your setup within ten minutes. If they aren't there by that time the possibility of calling one is rapidly reduced. Bobcats on the other hand take their own sweet time coming in. Twenty minutes is not a long time for a bobcat to take to come just several hundred yards.

The best example of how long it takes a bobcat to come to a call was my first experience with one of them. I was set up for coyotes in a small rock rim, just under a ridge with a fairly heavy stand of juniper on the ridge and below my position in a draw. The juniper had been browsed by the deer so a fifty to seventy yard coyote shot was going to be fairly easy.

There was a big, tall sagebrush flat across a second small draw about two hundred yards away. Immediately after I turned on the caller, six or seven deer stood up in the sage and looked straight at my position. They had seen me move into position, but felt well hidden at that distance in the heavy cover. Having deer stand up and look at a caller happens quite often, especially when the hunter is calling on winter ranges.

On this occasion, all of a sudden the deer looked uphill, away from me. Great, here comes Mr. 'Yote, I thought, and I began to watch for the coyote. Nothing showed. It should have taken the coyote less than two minutes to cover the head

One of the pleasant surprises of hunting coyotes is that other predators, like to bobcat, will sometimes respond to your call.

ends of the two draws, even if he was coming in at a slow trot. Sometimes they stop to see if they can see what is working on the rabbit to have the rodent put up such a commotion, but generally they are fairly quick to come into view.

As soon as the deer gave me the direction the critter was coming from, I moved slightly to get into a good shooting position. For the next ten minutes the dying rabbit blues was softly played over the M512. No coyote showed. The problem was, the deer were still looking up the hill at something getting closer to me. The deer did not move, but whatever was coming into my setup was taking its time. Finally, after another ten minutes of calling, the deer appeared to be looking right at me, but I sure could not see anything but the countryside and the deer.

Finally, I decided to shut off the caller as I was running out of tape. With the movement of my left hand to the turn off

Mule deer like these feeding in heavy willows provide a substantial part of the coyote prey base in most of the western states.

button, a bobcat took off at a full run from under the closest juniper tree, maybe twenty to twenty-five feet from my position. Unluckily for the bobcat I realized what it was immediately. It happened to be bobcat season and my wallet had an unused tag in it. The problem was, my adrenalin was working big time!

The first round was the typical buck fever shot of maybe twenty-five yards with nothing but bobcat in the scope. The dirt kicked up at least seven or eight feet in front of my intended target, and maybe that's why I even got a second shot. The critter stopped and was looking at the new hole in the dirt just in front. With all the control I could muster, the crosshairs finally settled on fur. My first bobcat hit the dust.

My point is, if you are in bobcat country and see some fresh cat sign, you may want to play that rabbit tape at least

Sometimes you get something into the caller bigger than a coyote. Jerry Russell with a 6½-year-old male mountain lion.

twenty minutes. The cottontail tape is far better for bobcats than the jackrabbit tape, too.

The red fox is also expanding its range throughout the United States. Ten years ago the only place I knew of any red fox in eastern Oregon was in the agricultural areas of Malheur County. Today these critters range over most of the agriculture areas. They have been west of the Cascades for a long time.

Coyotes and red fox usually do not coexist. The coyotes will defend their territory and run the red fox out.

That does not mean that these critters don't find niches in some locations to live. Areas of heavy cover close to towns will provide enough habitat for red fox to live and reproduce. They also come to a dying rabbit call, almost as fast as a slow coyote.

The best single word to describe a red fox approach to a caller's position is "paranoid." They come in fairly quickly, using all the available cover. If they see nothing suspicious they will keep coming, but with the first sign of danger they are history — even faster than a coyote. The coyote will stop with the distress yelp on the howler for a second look. Not a red fox.

These are just little extras to add some spice to your every day coyote hunting. They also add to your enjoyment and dreams at night.

LISTING OF BOOKS